Copyright © Allen Mbengeranwa 2015

Restaurant Exit Plan: How to obtain the Maximum Valuation

ISBN: 978-1-326-14987-1

Disclaimer and Legal Notice

While all attempts have been made to verify the information provided in this publication, neither the Author nor the Publisher assumes any responsibility for errors, omissions or contradictory interpretation of the subject matter herein. This publication is not intended for use as a source of any form of legal, financial, emotional, personal or accounting advice. The content is not a substitute or replacement of sound professional, insured advice. Please make up your own mind or engage the services of an individual or organisation willing to accept the responsibility which the author and publisher clearly will not, under any and all possible circumstances. The publisher wishes to let it be known and accepted that the information and illustrations contained herein may be subject to different geographical rules, regulations and laws. All users are advised to verify and determine what local rules, regulations and laws that their independent restaurant or business may be subject to. The reader or purchaser of this work assumes all responsibility for the use of these materials and information. Please accept and understand all local official and professional guides, rules, laws and regulations that govern your chosen business activity.

Table of Contents

Table of Figures 3
PREFACE 4
INTRODUCTION 5
Restaurant Value 9
The Restaurant Accounting Cycle 14
    Stock management 16
    Sales Management 16
The Restaurant Chart of Accounts (COA) 18
Category Accounts 20
Restaurant Accounting Software Applications 25
From Paper to Cloud 28
Computerised Software Applications Options 33
Juggling the Books 40
Restaurant Financial Performance Analyses 45
    Quick Ratio 51
    Current Ratio 52
    Asset Usage Ratios 52
'Beware the Ides of Restaurant Financial Analysis' 62
Restaurant Investment Appraisal 67
Restaurant Payback Technique 73
Return on Restaurant Investment Technique 75
Parting Note 78

Table of Figures

Figure 1 The Restaurant Accounting Cycle 15
Figure 2 The Restaurant Chart of Accounts 19
Figure 3 Restaurant Chart of Accounts Requirements 22
Figure 4 How to create your own coding for Restaurant C.O.A 23
Figure 5 An Example of a list of Restaurant Chart of Accounts 24
Figure 6 Restaurant Journal Characteristics 26
Figure 7 An example of Computerised leg-work 32
Figure 8 Restaurateur: Buyer Beware 35
Figure 9 Restaurant System launch and Personalisation 38
Figure 10 Moving From manual to Computerised Accounts .. 39
Figure 11 Identified Cash Forms 41
Figure 12 Restaurant Cash Handling Tasks 44
Figure 13 Restaurant Financial Performance Analysis 47
Figure 14 Restaurant Profitability Ratios 49
Figure 15 Restaurant Liquidity Ratios 50
Figure 16 Cash Flow Motto 53
Figure 17 Average Debt Collection Period 54
Figure 18 Rate of Stock Turnover 55
Figure 19 Other Restaurant Turnovers 56
Figure 20 Relationship between Sales and Fixed Assets 57
Figure 21 Relationship between Sales and Asset Values 59
Figure 22 Application of Restaurant Financial Ratios 62
Figure 23 Restaurant Appraisal Assumptions 69
Figure 24 Restaurant Investment Appraisal Techniques 70
Figure 25 Return on Investment 75

PREFACE

Caveat Venditor. Restaurant Exit Plan proposes an ideal method of operating day-to-day with Value Realisation in mind. In order to succeed, it is vital to understand the key component of a good financial Exit. Looking after the interests of whoever is coming in next is not only common courtesy, but also more likely to lead to a good high value clean break.

Your restaurant needs a strong illustration of accounting figures. This is important as it plays a pivotal role in any good Restaurant Exit plan. With that in mind, I will walk you through how to correctly understand and communicate financially for your best interests.

The objective is to make it easy, when you are ready to Exit for others to understand your restaurant business. As a seller, you may not be bound to volunteer negative information however; any potential buyer will go digging for anything that may pose a potential risk to their investment financial or otherwise.

There is no specific order in which to go through this book. The recommendation is that the readers asses for themselves where they are comfortable and start from there. However, it may be useful to treat the work as a starting point that will enable positive decision making. For a greater insight, the Restaurant Exit Plan builds an understanding that includes the very beginning and does not assume or take prior knowledge of finance or accounting for granted.

INTRODUCTION

Normally, the value of a restaurant will remain largely locked inside the business until the restaurateur finds someone willing to solidify that value by paying good money for it.

It is for this reason, Value Realisation, that many a Restaurateur dreams of selling their beloved restaurant and migrating to a faraway beach. At times, perhaps the Restaurateur may wish to hand over the reins to a family member safe in the knowledge that their baby is in good hands.

The reality is that you only get the opportunity to sell a restaurant once. When your business is sold, hopefully for a great price, it will probably mark the end of an era. The Restaurant Exit Plan door is fitted with an alarm and only leads one way: OUT.

Perhaps the Restaurateur may start again or try something different later. Chef and Restaurateur Piere Koffman is a good example of this journey. Having sold Le Tante Claires' original home in 1998 and then reappeared with Pierre Koffman at the Berkeley many years later.

Bankers and Venture Capitalists believe there are many ways to value a business but restaurants tend to have more emphasis put on the Accounting Valuation.

Naturally the Restaurateur will want to receive the maximum possible valuation and this is certainly easier and possible when the potential buyer is full of confidence with regards to the business.

Therefore, a clear set of detailed accounts and up to date databases of customers, suppliers and staff plus long term rolling contracts, if any, will be essential.

Good accounting practices from the beginning will help the buyer feel comfortable and reassured that the business model and all key aspects such as recipes and costs of ingredients, which are vital for restaurant continuity will still be in place once they sign on the proverbial dotted line and the money has safely left their account and is nesting neatly in the Restaurateur personal account.

Good accounts and accounting or bookkeeping practices are therefore vital when trying to portray a professional image.

It may also be a requirement in the future for the Restaurateur to plan for any number of taxes including Personal, Corporate or Capital Gains Tax.

The above is made easier through the employment of a good Accountant who can use good quality information that you will have provided. This is great for the restaurant business as it saves on professional fees and has the added benefit of impressing any potential buyer.

A distinct lack of Accounting or Bookkeeping knowledge may slow the Restaurateur down and prove to be costly through mistakes and time wasted trying to retrospectively acquire such knowledge.

The book *Restaurant Financial Management: Introduction to Accounting and for independent Restaurants* contains great descriptions and definitions for Bookkeeping as well as Accounting.

Bookkeeping and accounting are both relevant and important as they provide a paper chase to enable the Restaurateur to analyze any failures and identify success.

As you are probably aware, there are different accounting methods and the most relevant to Restaurants are Cash Accounting or Accrual Accounting. Essentially the fundamental difference between the two relates to the moment in which sales and purchases are recorded or when they 'Hit' the books.

With the Cash Accounting, as the name suggests, transactions are only recorded when actual cash or near cash changes hands. In the later, Accrual Accounting, the emphasis is on recording transactions when either the sales or purchases are completed.

Accounting is a system of recording and processing financial data. With that in mind, the restaurants Accounting Period is therefore the amount of time over which the restaurants financial information is being monitored.

It is important to appreciate time in this manner as it comes in handy when constructing and during consultations on your personal Restaurant Exit Plan.

Restaurant Value

Restaurant Value is created when the restaurant earns a return on your investment in excess of the cost of capital. The Restaurateur will come up with business strategies in an attempt to achieve value maximization through the restaurants activities.

As the owner and to a lesser extent a manager, your business strategy determines how the restaurant positions itself in its local environment to achieve a distinct and unique competitive advantage.

The restaurants financial statements illustrate the rewards to be enjoyed as well as the economic consequences of operating within the hospitality industry.

Ordinarily, every restaurant undertakes activities which are proprietary in nature and under normal circumstances, disclosing these activities in great detail could be detrimental to the restaurants competitive position. There seems to be great value in safe guarding some secrets.

However, when formulating your Restaurant Exit Plan, you have to transform the business into a market stall where all business activities and the accounting systems used to produce the financial statements are temporarily on display.

Your insider knowledge as the Restaurateur needs to be translated into true information without distortion and noise for any of the outsiders formulating an entry plan.

Should your Restaurant Exit Plan have too much distortion and noise, the result may lead to 'discounting' of your accounting performance and ultimately negatively impact your Value Realisation.

Ideally, you need financial and management information that adds value by improving a potential restaurant investors understanding of your restaurants current performance and its future prospects.

Incidentally, the preceding statement is what the Restaurant Exit Plan holds true to its heart and central to your success.

There are a few ways of analyzing your restaurant. When you are thinking of leaving, you may not worry about the business' future. However, a prospective buyer may wish to analyse the restaurant focusing on forecasting the restaurants future. This will focus mainly on financial statement forecasting and restaurant valuation.

When you formulate your Restaurant Exit plan, it will serve you well to remember that the value of your restaurant is a function of its future cash flow performance or the current book value of equity and any future Return on Capital Employed as well as likely future growth.

Restaurants are usually classified as small businesses, the level of detail or amount of work put into some activities like valuation has to be proportionate. It is vanity to employ the highest rated professionals such as Bankers, Accountants and Solicitors only to have their fees amount to a higher monetary value than your restaurant.

Hans Christian Andersen may have penned "The Emperor's New Clothes" with a moral message in mind. Today a small child walking along London's Chelsea Harbour may marvel at the yachts owned by professional financial advisors. Would it be unreasonable for the child to turn around and ask, "so where are their customers yachts?".

Accounting analysis provides an acceptable unbiased estimate of your restaurants current book value and Return on Capital Employed.

Your Restaurant Exit Plan requires appropriate use of financial and accounting tools which you are required to be familiar with as well as their relevance to your restaurant concept.

Boring as it may sound; you have to evaluate the extent to which your restaurants accounting system and policies capture the underlying business reality.

Normally, most restaurants have no separation between ownership and management as the two are typically one and the same person. In spite of this, financial statements remain the method by which your potential buyers keep track of the restaurants financial situation.

Let's not forget that getting out of a restaurant can be as easy as contacting an agent who will charge you to erect a 'for sale' sign and have you out of there in a matter of days. You could even pay for a one line advertisement in the local paper and that could just as easily do the job. Besides making use of the internet, word of mouth can also have the same desired effect and have you 'cashing in' just as easy.

Accounting rules are said to require a certain amount of minimum disclosure. As a Restaurateur, you have a surprisingly wide spectrum of choice or freedom in the degree of openness you engage.

Therefore, disclosure quality is an important aspect of the restaurants' accounting quality.

If you intend to unlock the sweet fruits of your labour by executing a Restaurant Exit Plan, then it may be to your advantage to adequately disclose information that will enable others to assess your restaurants business situation and its economic consequences.

You need to properly explain your restaurants performance and keys to success. The degree to which it appears that you are forthcoming with bad news and reasons for poor performance may put you in good stead.

Executing your Restaurant Exit Plan will involve questions on how you handle professional dysphoria. Areas of discomfort or distress due to your socially expected professional status and the social roles that are associated with being a professional Restaurateur will be easier to deal with by employing good accounting information.

What do you really want or better still, deserve, from the restaurant business?

Imagine yourself standing in the midst of the beauty of the Glens of Scotland in their entire splendor. Flowing next to you is one of the many clear rivers glistening in the mid-morning sun. Spare a thought for the rocks on the riverbed that will never know when it's raining.

With the above in mind, as you keep your nose on the restaurant grinding stone, be aware that you have choices. One of the choices may involve making a relatively large amount of money. If you have not done so already, then take a moment. A brief but important moment, to lift your head above the parapet. In order to appreciate your accounting systems as a vital part of the Restaurant Exit Plan.

The Restaurant Accounting Cycle

The restaurants accounts will therefore cover a length of time, a month for example. However, the accounts are also prepared at other significant periods in time. Specifically, quarterly accounts and Restaurant Financial Year End Accounts. At the end of each accounting period, the restaurants books are subsequently closed and simultaneously opened for the next accounting period, as time has never been known to stand still, even for the Professional Chef.

The above therefore means that Restaurant has an accounting cycle over which the process repeats itself per period.

Figure 1 The Restaurant Accounting Cycle

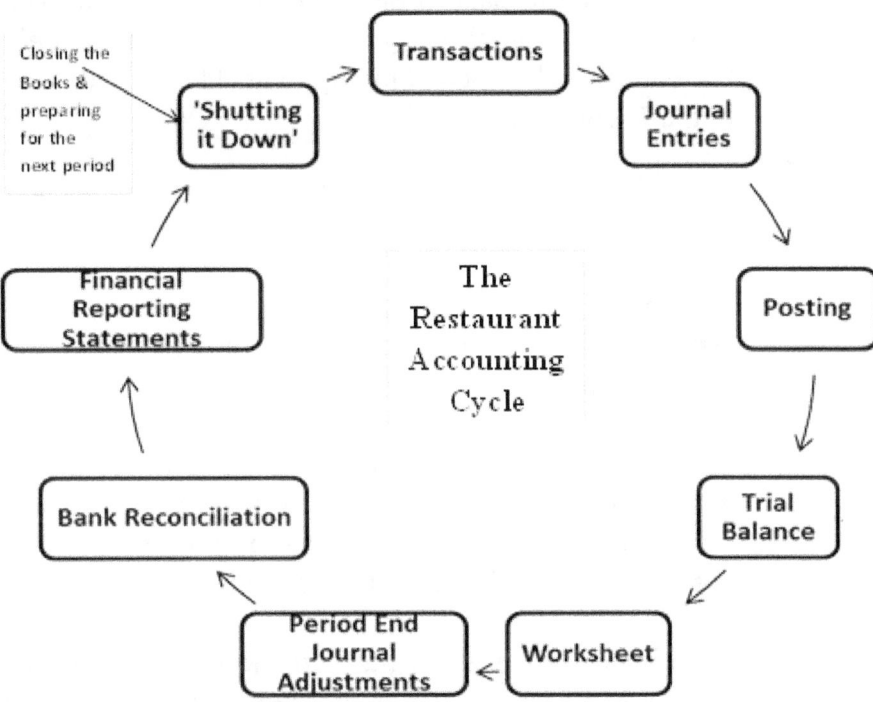

It's not a matter of simply heading for the exit door when you decide to cash in on your Restaurant. There has to be a plan. The idea is that you run the restaurant knowing that one day you want to seek professional advice and head for the Exit.

Unfortunately for some, this means that while running the establishment, you need to use a good accounting system to illustrate great stock and sales management. The system needs to be organized and easy to use. Traditionally, a Chart of Accounts (COA) is used to paint a picture of what's going on with all the restaurants' financial data and how it works. At some point the Books need to be opened for a potential buyer and their advisors or the Tax people.

Stock management

The Restaurant Exit Plan generates better results in terms of a higher valuation when accounting records show good stock management.

Tracking the cost of restaurant stock helps to manage the profit potential of the business. While you are busy heading for the Exit Only sign, the person bringing value to your restaurant has a keen eye on the future direction of the business.

Restaurant costs need to be more closely managed in order to identify and highlight trends plus help the potential buyer make informed decisions about adjustments, sooner rather than later. Costs that later spiral out of control have been known to destroy many a good Restaurateur's reputation and quite simply annihilate the perceived value.

Sales Management

Turnover is a great value. Normally it's an important figure. However, anyone serious about entering your restaurant business and allowing you to exit will be interested in your accounting records, especially the fact that all the sales numbers are easy to see and for them to understand.

Therefore, it is imperative that you also monitor customer activity. The effectiveness of any discounts and the impact of product returns such as customer dissatisfaction with plates of food or open wine, is also a level of detail that will assure qualified potential buyers.

Furthermore, not just for you but the potential buyer as well, there will be an appreciation of the impact of price changes; market conditions; local competitors on sales weaknesses. These can all be illustrated in the accounting information.

For the Exit Plan, Sales Management is used to essentially identify the underlying systems in order to deal with the real causes of problems.

As an example, an increase in restaurant waste due to higher than average customer returns is usually a good indicator that more research is needed.

To allow you to exit, a Potential Entrant may conclude, upon discovery through your accounting information, that product quality is declining and/or employees are mis-selling and therefore a new supplier is needed and/or staff is to undergo new training under their stewardship in the near future. Your Exit Plan is still on track.

The Restaurant Chart of Accounts (COA)

This is the DNA or roadmap of your bookkeeping and accounting system. It is a list of all the accounts or headings that the restaurant has and specifies what type of restaurant transactions are recorded into each account.

The COA of the restaurant is useful for all staff and not just the Bookkeeper or Accountant, as individual codes can be used for invoices or other transactions to indicate which account these transactions should be recorded. This is particularly important for refunds and returns. Operating in this manner makes it easy for a new buyer coming in.

The system or organization of accounts for the restaurant revolves around the Balance Sheet and the Profit and Loss Statements to establish its central structure and its characteristics. In essence, it's a mirror of the restaurant operations.

Figure 2 The Restaurant Chart of Accounts

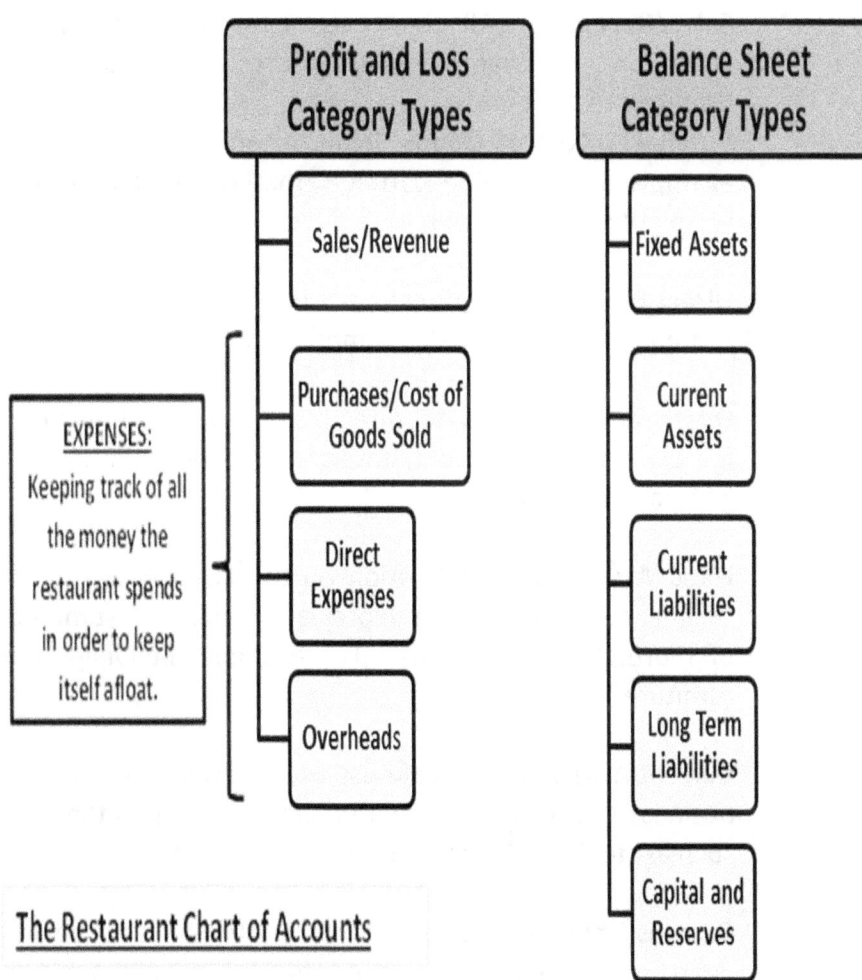

Category Accounts

Sales/Revenue. All the revenue streams coming into your restaurant, for example Sales; Interest Received; Discounts and Credit Notes.

Purchases/Cost of Goods Sold. All the trading purchases. For example Stock related carriage, that is direct costs involved in selling to customers, purchase discounts and credit notes

Direct Expenses. Any direct costs involved in the sale of goods, for example, Labour and Sales commission.

Overheads. Expenses not directly attributable to the Cost of Sales, for example wages; rent; rates; annual depreciation; Insurance; general advertising.

Fixed Assets. All information on the Fixed Assets including the original cost and ongoing depreciation with an estimated lifespan of more than 12 months. For example: buildings; stoves and furniture.

Current Assets. Includes almost any asset owned by the restaurant business that has an estimated short life of less than 12 months such as stock; Cash and Bank current account balance.

Current Liabilities. Mostly liabilities that have to be paid in the near future in particular: Creditors; VAT Liability and Short Term Loans. This also includes interest payable in less than 12 months.

Long Term Liabilities. The rest of the restaurants Liabilities that do not have to be paid in the near future such as long term creditors and mortgages of more than 12 months.

Capital and Reserves. This shows how the restaurant was financed. Contains information on: the Capital Introduced; Share Capital; Unused Reserves and the Current Years Profit or Loss.

Figure 3 Restaurant Chart of Accounts Requirements

Restaurant Chart of Accounts Requirements

ACCOUNT: lists the title/name of the accounts

TYPE: type of account for example Asset, Liability, Income, Cost Of Goods Sold or expense

DESCRIPTION: description of the type of transactions that should be recorded in the account

ACCOUNT NUMBER: Coding charges

Figure 4 How to create your own coding for Restaurant C.O.A

• HOW TO CREATE YOUR OWN CODING FOR RESTAURANT C.O.A.

• Fixed Assets	0,000	>	0,999	**NOTES**
• Asset Accounts	1,000	>	1,999	It is recommended that you leave loads of space between Accounts as you may need to add new ones during the year or your Restaurant Business Model evolves
• Liability Accounts	2,000	>	2,999	
• Equity Accounts	3,000	>	3,999	
• Sales Accounts	4,000	>	4,999	
• Purchases	5,000	>	5,999	
• Direct Expenses	6,000	>	6,999	
• Overheads	7,000	>	7,999	
• Miscellaneous	8,000	>	8,999	

Restaurant Exit Plan: How to obtain the Maximum Valuation

Figure 5 An Example of a list of Restaurant Chart of Accounts

An example of a List of Restaurant Chart of Accounts

Number	Type	Name	Description
6001	Expense	Advertising	
6002	Expense	Insurance	
6003	Expense	Lease/hire purchase	
6004	Expense	Legal fees	
6005	Expense	professional fees	
6006	Expense	Bank Charges	
6007	Expense	Interest charges	
6008	Expense	Office Equipment	
6009	Expense	Sales/Purchase Tax	
6010	Expense	Rent	
6011	Expense	Telephone/Internet	
6012	Expense	Utilities	
6013	Expense	Carriage/Postage	
6014	Expense	Trade Shows	
6015	Expense	Casual Wages	
6016	Expense	Travel	
6017	Expense	Entertainment	

Restaurant Accounting Software Applications

The beginning of the accounting process or Chart of Accounts is usually the journal entry. As far as starting the process of accurately communicating financial information, the journal is probably the best place to begin.

Hopefully your restaurant will have hundreds of transactions to manage. This is a preferred nightmare to have than the flip side of little or no transactions. Without a descent process or system, communication and mistakes may lead to frustration with the later neigh on impossible to detect should the books not balance, for any reason.

The rules of bookkeeping require every transaction to have both a debit and credit. A system of journals allows the restaurant to have a starting point or a transactions point of entry into the system.

Ordinarily, bookkeeping standards dictate that each journal has the following Characteristics:

Figure 6 Restaurant Journal Characteristics

Restaurant Journal Characteristics

Chronological Referance Number	Date of Transaction	Date of entry into System	Accounts to which the transaction was posted by way of Debit or Credit	The Source material used for developing the transaction

The objective is to keep track of incoming cash and also follow the journey of any restaurant outgoing cash. Both of those actions can also be done using journals as the point of original entry.

It is important to correctly track outgoing and incoming cash carefully. Most restaurants deal in cash and as we are all only human, it is not only a good idea but a necessity to have a number of accurate checks and balances to ensure that cash is carefully handled and recorded.

In the current climate, it seems that only fit and proper persons are allowed to carry out business activities, especially those handling cash. Increasing the government requests that Restaurateurs, when requested, provide evidence that they are not money laundering or conducting business with entities considered enemies of the state.

The Daddy of modern-day bookkeeping as we currently know it, Luca Pacioli, recommended as far back as 1494 that 'One should not sleep until the Debits equal the Credits'. Well, One should also not sleep unless they have records to show compliance with current statutes and government directives, might I add.

From Paper to Cloud

At the end of the accounting period, the cycle needs to end and the books closed. It is far easier for the software to total, accurately all columns and then the journals into the General Ledger and other places without the need for individual error prone human entries.

At the moment, the entire accounting process has been assumed to be easily handled by the restaurateur manually. A computer software program or application does essentially the same, with added benefits.

Many a restaurateur would assume that the computer leads to less information handling. However, as paper work is fragile and incredibly susceptible to loss or irreparable damage, journals are usually kept to a minimum.

The above paperwork has the limiting factor of preventing the restaurateur from producing detailed financial data as this is based on a reduced sampling pool for the information.

In addition, data manipulation is also hindered as a result of fewer journals being kept, there is a significant reduction in the parameters available and hence the number of possible scenarios or variations is limited.

Restaurant Software applications not only reduce the time spent on accounting tasks but also allow for more accurate recording and duplication of financial information.

Some transactions will need more than just a Debit and corresponding Credit entry. For example, a customer is sold a bottle of wine, a debit entry, which later turns out to be ruined. When the restaurant offers a customer refund to the less than satisfied guest, this transaction is posted to the customer account as a credit of the meal sold. Then the Accounts Receivable is also credited and finally the Customer Refund/Return account as a debit entry.

To make life more fun, applying a common, unique reference to the above transaction allows the Restaurateur to be fully aware of exactly what is going on without being lost, confused or short changed.

A 'ballet' similar to the above also takes place should the Chef or Restaurant manager wish to return a product to a supplier. There may be no cash movement or change of hands with regards to the transaction.

As far as headaches go, a software program is available to accurately keep track of who owes who what where and when, in addition to how plus why.

In terms of accounting, the difference between one restaurant and the next is phenomenal. The accounting process involving first posting to the journals, followed by the individual customer of supplier accounts and then the General Ledger can be time consuming.

It is also possible that the Restaurateur may find accounting mind numbingly boring as the same or similar transactions need to be entered many times over. Some people say life is too short so it's a good thing that the computer software application does some of the repetition for you, automatically, so to speak.

Restaurants experience many types of transactions. As a result, the manner or method in which this information is entered into the accounting system varies. By using computer software, the Restaurateur is able to use one variable, such as supplier name, and instantly view all the current invoices or credit notes.

At this point, it is possible to update an invoice payment record while simultaneously updating the Bank Current Account journal, Sales Tax Account, General Ledger and Profit and Loss Statement. Clicking on "SAVE and CLOSE" completes the entire process.

Alternatively, tracking a cash receipt through the software application program also automatically updates:
- The Bank Current Account with a debit for the appropriate amount
- Accounts Receivable is credited with the appropriate amount
- Specific Customer Account is credited with the exact same amount.

- The Cash Receipt is instantly matched to the corresponding original Restaurant Sales.

Using a computerized program allows the Restaurateur to delegate, in confidence as the possibility of errors is significantly reduced.

The above is possible because most of the data entry into the journals and ledgers is through standardized forms that do not necessarily need the user to grasp the ins and outs of debits and credits for instance, as the computer software application 'takes care' of everything.

The NET result is that the Restaurateur is able to 'focus' on other perhaps more important aspects of the restaurant such as customer service and promotion. However, more time on the golf course or at the gym is also an option.

As for the Restaurant EXIT PLAN, it would be better for the process and even expected that the books are computerized.

Figure 7 An example of Computerised leg-work

- Total recall of specific products
- Automatic printing of Remittance advice
- Auto Complete of Customer information
- Update Supplier Account completed payments
- Unique Supplier invoice Number
- Debit Credit Control Account Adjust total to Supplier
- Automatic Date Entry
- Credit Bank Current Account, Decrease funds
- Calculation of Discounts/ Credit Notes and TAX
- Consistant Format/ Appearance
- Automatic Sub Totals and Final Total

Restaurant Supplier Payment

Computerised Software Applications Options

Progress in the world of computers has meant that Restaurateurs are faced with an increasing number of options as far as Accounting software goes. Not only is there an increase in amount and styles, there is a significant reduction in the price of available software.

It may be unbelievable; however, the price starts at Free for the bottom end which is phenomenal. Therefore, price does not seem to be a barrier to the use of software in the Restaurant Exit Plan.

There are some important and necessary aspects to consider. Please seek legal professional insured advice with most aspects of the restaurant, especially financial. It sounds obvious but it is a necessary evil.

Apparently, accounting as a career choice is guaranteed to decline in the near future as current technological trends show a significant rise in the use of Software, in place of the human function.

Of great importance is the need to assess your needs and to establish exactly what you want the restaurant accounting software to do. Almost all software is capable of communicating the necessary information pivotal to a great Restaurant Exit Plan.

At the moment, it is not hard to see what's available and how much it costs. Most of the information is available online. The options are vast and are based on:

1. Traditional Compact Disk products
2. Online paperless download onto Restaurant Computer System and registration/activation
3. Cloud based Software Login

Increasingly, Generic Accounting Software Applications are facing stiff competition from industry –specific options. These specialists are addressing unique sector issues.

In addition to specialization, there seems to be a trend towards producing more complex restaurant accounting output from even more simple input options, relative to yester year.

Figure 8 Restaurateur: Buyer Beware

Aside from bookkeeping, accounting policy is affected by legislation, which may change on an annual basis. Therefore, any chosen software needs to have the ability to update standard political decisions such as VAT rate and Customs and Excise Duty.

Once in a while, there are significant legislative changes that divert from decades of practice. More recently, the European Union ruling that international Web based companies pay Corporation tax at the rate set by the Governments in the country in which the sales are generated.

The above is significant because should the Restaurateur choose to buy wine from a company registered in the Republic of Ireland, if based in the United Kingdom, the rate will be a local 20 per cent as opposed to traditional Irish 15 per cent. This change affects buyers as well as sellers and needs to be accurately reported in the restaurants accounting practices.

More significantly, there is a change in user expectations of software functions and technology perceptions of the current restaurant industry working population. Paperless invoicing from accounting software may soon be de rigueur

The level of pre and post purchase support has also risen significantly. Training is available to restaurants from the software provider or third parties such as local colleges, at a cost. There is also an expectation of human support either online or via the telephone, in addition to the user manual.

Considering how easy it would be to migrate between different restaurant accounting systems is also important. This is because the restaurant and Restaurateur may evolve and mature over time. Perhaps even more important is making sure that any potential buyer will not find it difficult to assimilate your financial data into their preferred system.

Stock control is very important to a restaurant. It is easy for the Chef to order ingredients on a daily basis depending on the season and sales levels for example. However, stock control has to be translated into financial data not only for monitoring and historic analysis but also to prove to a buyer the necessary information to make an informed decision.

It seems easy to manage the restaurant budget from invoice totals alone. Unfortunately, this practice means that the software is not working on raw data but totals which reduce analysis and the level of detail in information communications.

In conclusion, how much information your software can work with or handle could prove vital. So how does the paper world merge into the world of Cloud-based computing? How then do the two co-exist for your restaurant and play a vital role in your Exit plan? Perhaps is necessary to illustrate how it all flows together.

Figure 9 Restaurant System launch and Personalisation

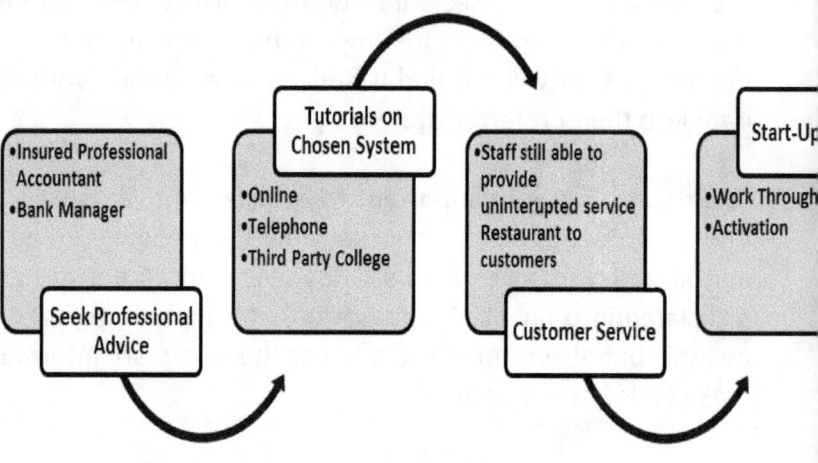

Figure 10 Moving From manual to Computerised Accounts

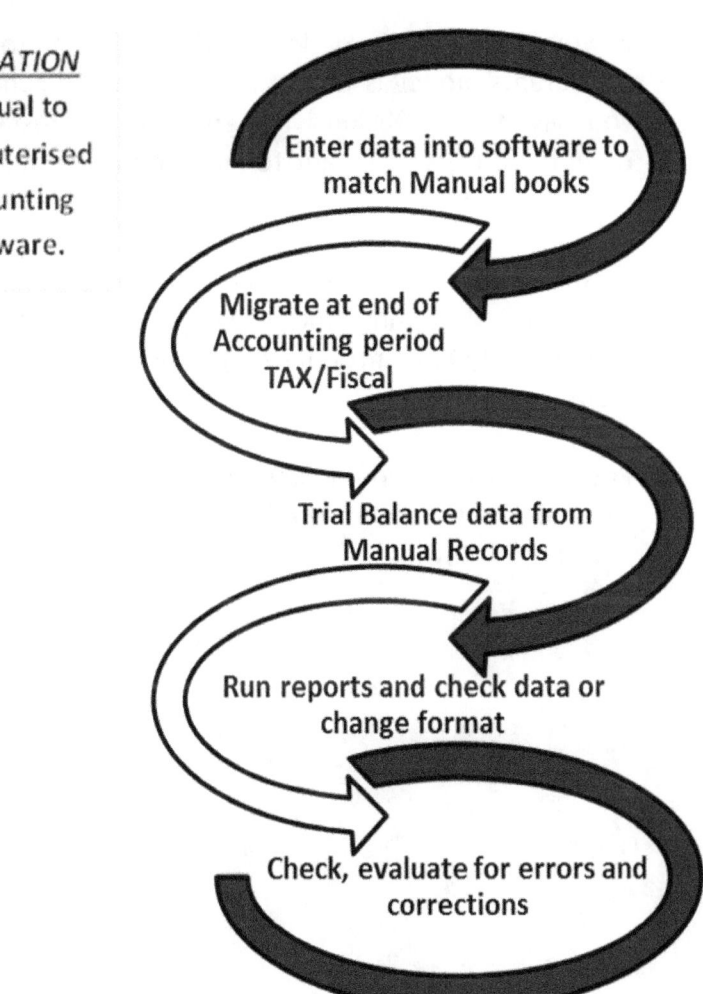

Juggling the Books

In your Restaurant Exit Plan, it is important to show that the restaurants money is where it should be and coming from where you say it is. Obviously when selling a restaurant business, potential buyers will want to know how the business was doing and why.

Cash, in its many guises is the life blood of any Restaurateurs business. Accepting and loving all forms of cash confers a responsibility to control the subject and keeping a good recording system.

Prior to executing your restaurant exit plan, it helps to ensure that cash does not walk out the front or back doors once it arrives as any of the following:

Figure 11 Identified Cash Forms

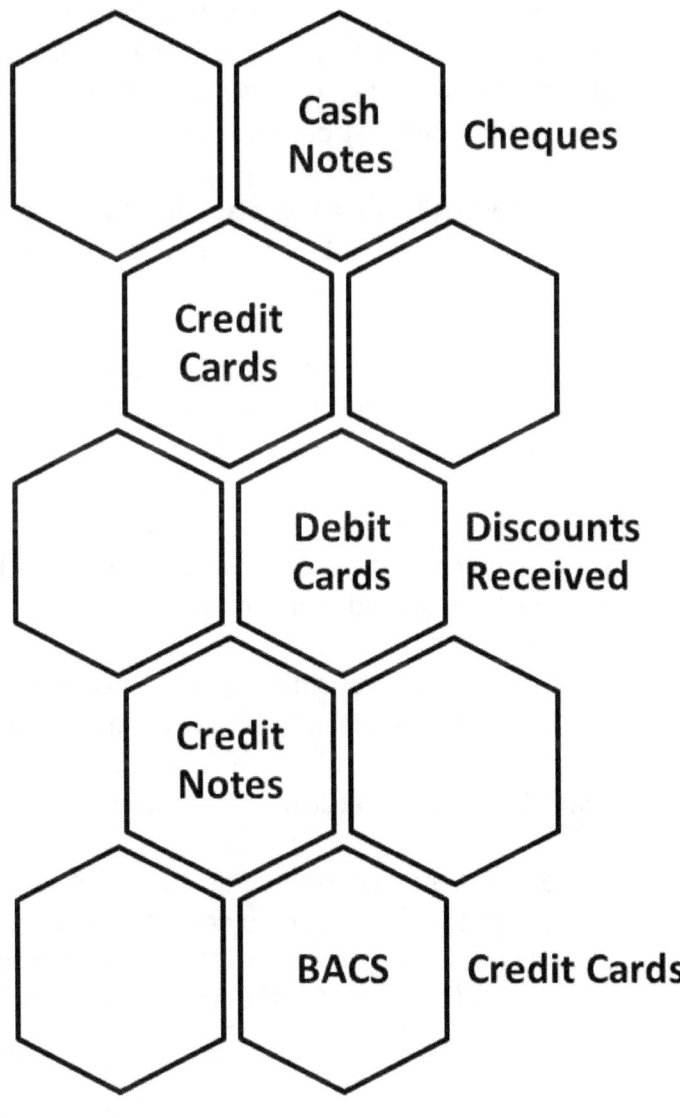

The levels of cash control range from Lackadaisical to the more stereotypical Tightwad. Most Restaurateurs presumably operate at a level which they are comfortable enough to allow employees the flexibility to sell to customers and provide vital customer service for repeat patronage.

Even though Tightwad is also the name of a small village in Missouri, in this instance it represents the extreme end of 'Scrooge-like' financial management.

The assumption is that too Lax a control system, not the anatomical kind, leads to a significant increase in the risk of theft or financial fraud. In some extreme cases, the restaurant can be purgative in terms of money and hemorrhage cash at a rate of knots, if left unchecked. Ever heard the one where the junior trainee charged a lucky customer one glass at £7 instead of a whole £7,000.00 bottle of Petrus?

The opposite is true, too tight an accounting based financial control system may lead to employees missing many opportunities to complete sales of additional beverages, for example or alienate valuable customers at significant cost to the Restaurateur.

There are basic controls that the Chef or Restaurateur can implement and is expected to demonstrate upon Exit that monitor incoming and outgoing cash. The controls will ensure that the restaurants funds are clearly documented and managed.

Monitoring the restaurants cash appears very different from tracing personal cash usage. However, despite interest from different stakeholders, the objective remains the same. All cash is expected to be properly protected and seen to be accurately accounted for using sound accounting principles.

As more people handle the restaurants cash, this one aspect, higher frequency of contact and increased probability due to larger sampling pool, makes the money more vulnerable to errors of judgment and less than accurate controls.

In terms of efficient day to day operations, it is not feasible to have only one person handling the cash as this is inefficient and likely to lead to loss of business as a result of terrible customer experience leading to loss of any potential repeat business. There may also be a knock on effect in terms of generating new customers as bad restaurant reviews turn potential customers to your competitors.

Normally cash also comes into the restaurant in many forms, often at the same time. The Restaurateur also needs to dispense cash in as many forms, again, possibly all at once. Subsequently, it may become awkward to correctly manage all these cash streams resulting in negative stressful situations and a bad restaurant environment.

These diverse cash handling scenarios alone may leave the Restaurateur with little or no opportunity to engage in other tasks or activities.

Figure 12 Restaurant Cash Handling Tasks

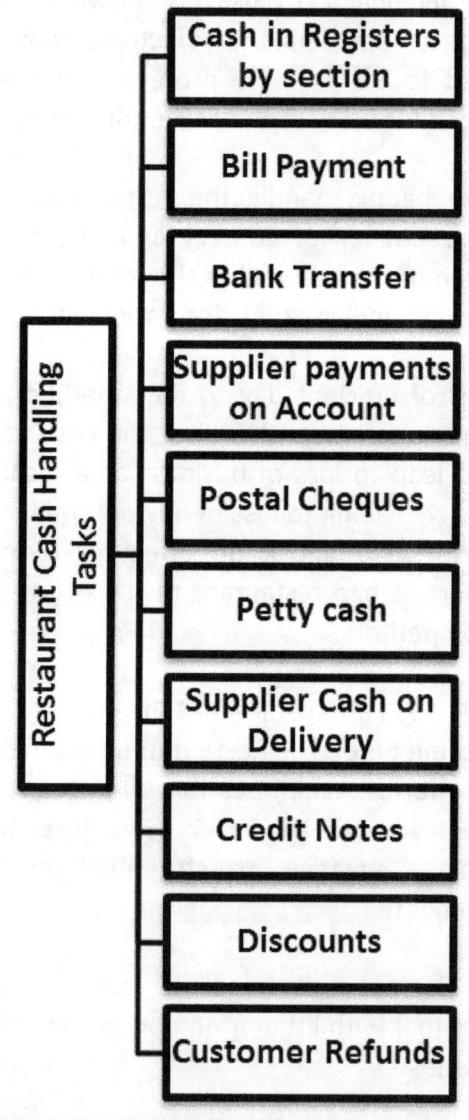

Restaurant Financial Performance Analyses

Critically looking at a restaurant using accounting information such as balance sheets and Profit and Loss statements is a good method of looking at how the restaurant performed in the past. It is perhaps important to bear in mind that for the Restaurateur, this information is historic in nature.

Anyone willing to facilitate your restaurant exit will instinctively try to evaluate and judge their participation in your process on your financial integrity.

Good restaurant financial records are an excellent indicator of how the Restaurateur managed the business in the past and can illustrate whether the performance was exceptional, atrocious or somewhere in between.

As with most forms of information, the restaurants financial records are based mostly on data summaries or compression. This state of affairs is universally acceptable simply because listing every item will not only be counterproductive but also useless as a method or form of communication.

Instead of conveying information, the data will simply form a list that is neither artistic nor practical or useful, even to the creator. The use of standard guidelines for financial information, although not necessarily compulsory, is considered good practice if other people are to be involved. Normally, you will need to file Tax or

Customs information of some sort and the relevant authorities have standardized assessment methods for what may or may not be due.

Most restaurant financial records contain the information as headlines or asset category types that leave out the finer details. Take the headline Assets for example, their composition and perhaps actual physical location among other distinguishing factors are not included.

The value at a point in historical time is used for financial records and not much else about the nature of the asset or liability.

Having said that, the restaurateur and other stakeholders accept that, although limited, financial records are the best method of communication in your restaurant exit plan. As everyone uses them, thus creating a level playing field, use can still be derived in order to keep an eye on the restaurants current performance, evaluate historic results and perhaps even anticipate or predict and future growth or unwelcome decline of the restaurant.

For the restaurants financial information to be useful as opposed to just a dusty collection of numbers, there needs to be some sort of analysis. Restaurant Analysis usually denotes to a practical method of physical discovery in which the financial information is interpreted or broken down into smaller results to reflect an initial desired understanding or interpretation.

Figure 13 Restaurant Financial Performance Analysis

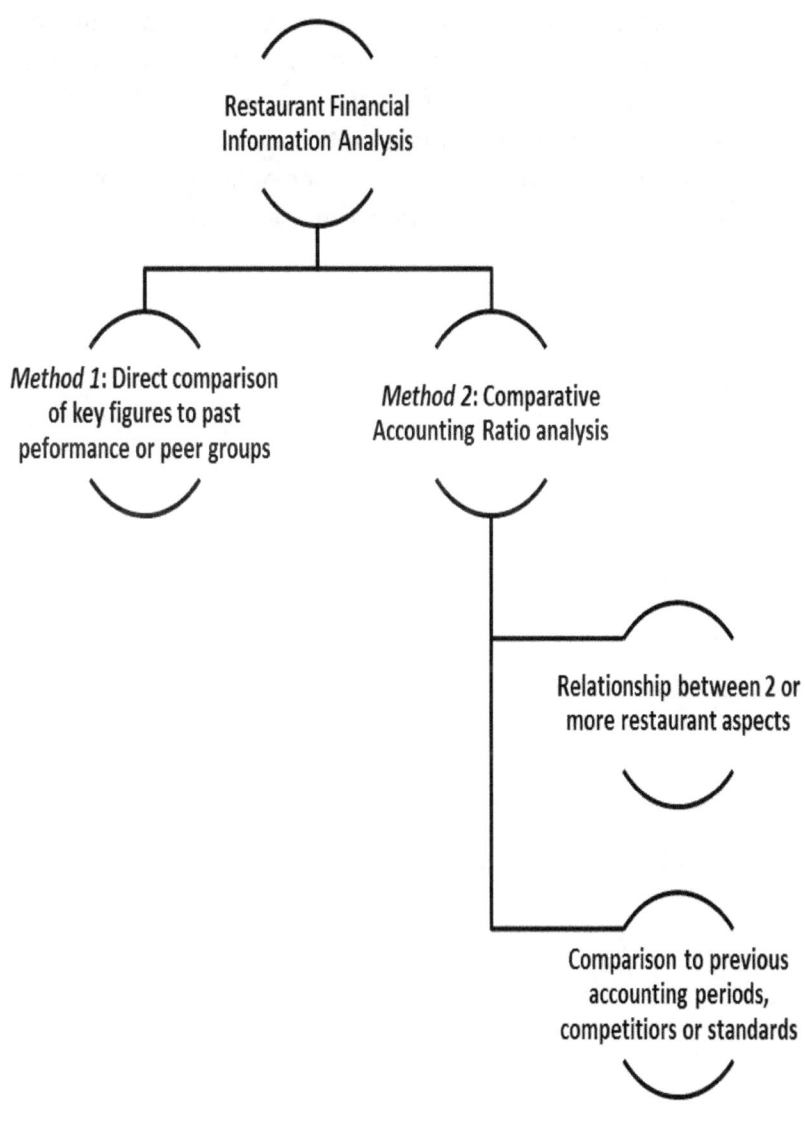

Method 1 has the unfortunate limitations of being rendered almost entirely useless if differences in accounting policies and procedures exist. Furthermore, the timing of transactions also affects the relevance of results as well. Another factor that also affects the outcome of this method is the size of the restaurant in terms of turnover or total number of staff employed. The use of absolute figures may mislead the user to irrelevant conclusions.

Figure 14 Restaurant Profitability Ratios

RESTAURANT PROFITABILITY RATIOS

1. Rate of Gross Profit = $\dfrac{\text{Gross Profit}}{\text{Sales}} \times 100$

2. Rate of Net Profit = $\dfrac{\text{Net Profit}}{\text{Sales}} \times 100$

3. ROCE = $\dfrac{\text{Net Proft BIT}}{\text{Capital employed}} \times 100$

4. Capital employed = Total Net assets

   or

   = Fixed assets - Deprecitation
   plus Current Assets - Current Liabilities

Where ROCE is Return On Captal Employed
BIT is Before Interest and Tax
CE is Capital Employed
NPBIT is Net Profit Before Interest and Tax

ROCE is the best of the four for profitability

$$\dfrac{\text{NPBIT}}{\text{CE}} \times 100 = \dfrac{\text{NPBIT}}{\text{Sales}} \times 100 \times \dfrac{\text{Sales}}{\text{CE}}$$

Figure 15 Restaurant Liquidity Ratios

RESTAURANT LIQUIDITY RATIOS

The pair indicate the solvency of the restaurant, they show whether the Restaurateur has enough money to pay creditors.

1. Current Ratio = $\dfrac{\underline{\text{Current Assets}}}{\text{Current Liabilities}}$

2. Quick Ratio = $\dfrac{\underline{\text{Current assets - Stocks - Investments}}}{\text{Current Liabilities}}$

The second ratio also known as the Acid Test which is a test or indicator of the Restaurants liquidity. The Quick Ratio or Acid Test is widely accepted as the best of liquidity ratios as it does not take into account Capital or value locked in Stock or the Restaurateurs short term investments. it shows the impact or ability of the restaurant to pay is short-term bills when due. these include Accruals and Wages.

Quick Ratio

If your restaurant is financially healthy, it will have Quick ratio of 1. Most independent restaurants will have a smaller ratio primarily because most customers pay in cash or near cash and credit lines tend to be short.

However, having said that, if the restaurant ratio exceeds 1 by a margin that is relatively too big in the industry by site size, it could be a possible sign that the Restaurateur is inefficient. A potential buyer or Investor may assume that this margin is because of over ordering as too much money may be tied up in stock.

On a personal level, this may not be a good sign for you as restaurants need a high stock turnover to maintain high quality standards. This may be an area where someone else feels they can come in and add value. The unfortunately, this possibility of improvement may lead to a lower valuation, rather than attracting a higher restaurant exit price.

The possible exception to the above is wine and other such beverages that benefit or are not affected by a short durability statement.

Essentially, assets with a good liquidity are easily convertible into cash.

Current Ratio

Normally, the restaurants current ratio has a value of 2, on average. As the Current ratio is also known as the Working Capital Ratio, if this value is low, it may be an indicator that your restaurant is edging towards insolvency. Oh dear.

On the other hand, the lesser of two evils, a high Working Capital value highlights that the Restaurateur is somewhat inefficient at the management of current assets and current liabilities. This may suite an outsider who believes they can implement the necessary changes and garner a great rate of return for themselves. It may not appeal to anyone seeking to facilitate your exit and acquire a low risk investment that does not need much tinkering, so to speak.

Asset Usage Ratios

Most restaurants have and need to own assets. Consumer trends, Chefs training or preferences mean that there are different types of equipment and other assets that he restaurant will acquire over time.

These assets are vitally important to your restaurant and the industry and the ratios indicate how efficiently the Restaurateur makes use of them in the business.

Before you complete your Restaurant Exit, whoever is coming in will want to be confident about the assets that you intend to leave behind.

The Restaurant Business Model is usually very simple and asset usage ratios are an excellent way of identifying how to improve efficiency and ensure greater profitability from current assets, especially Stocks and Debtors.

Restaurant Financial Management: Introduction to Accounting and finance for Independent Restaurants is a book that looks at assets for the restaurant in a financial and operational aspect. It also looks at areas such as waste and optimum asset usage especially with regard to staff.

Figure 16 Cash Flow Motto

> "Get Paid Fast and Pay you Debtors as Slow as Possible, but remember, Eggs have no Business Dancing with Stones."

The above quote is also a method of improving your restaurants liquidity position, if it is proving problematic. Please remember that all strategies are exercised with caution and scope for flexibility, ideally.

As with most aspects of the restaurant world, the possibilities are endless. However, a small handful of asset usage ratios are the most important and considered sufficient enough to paint an accurate picture.

Figure 17 Average Debt Collection Period

Average Debt Collection Period (ADCP)

$$ADCP = \frac{\text{Average Debtors}}{\text{Credit Sales}} \quad \text{or} \quad \frac{\text{Average Debtors}}{\text{Total Sales}}$$

where Average Debtors is $\dfrac{\text{Closing Debtors + Opening Debtors}}{2}$

The smaller the value for the restaurant, the better. Business average is assumed to be 45 days, which may be too long for most restaurants.

Figure 18 Rate of Stock Turnover

Rate of Stock Turnover (RST)

$$\text{RST} = \frac{\text{Cost of Sales}}{\text{Average Stock}}$$

where Average Stock is $\quad 1/2 \text{ (Opening + Closing) Stock}$

The result indicates the number of times the Restaurant turns over its stock per year.

The rate of Stock Turnover is more important for the restaurant if it is expressed in days.

$$\text{Rate of Stock Turnover (In Days)} = \frac{\text{Average Stock}}{\text{Cost of Sales}} \times 365$$

This Ratio of Stock Turnover needs to be seen as getting comparatively higher over time for Stock that is classified as food ingredients. Therefore it may be useful to use different figures for the Restaurant Ratio for Rate of Food Stock Turnover and Rate of Beverage Turnover as well as Rate of Other Stock Turnover such as cleaning and maintenance products.

Figure 19 Other Restaurant Turnovers

$$\text{Rate of food Turnover} = \frac{\text{Average Food Stock}}{\text{Cost of food Sales}} \times 365$$

$$\text{Rate of Beverage Turnover} = \frac{\text{Average Beverage Stock}}{\text{Cost of Beverage Sales}} \times 365$$

$$\text{Rate of Other Stock Turnover} = \frac{\text{Average Other Stock}}{\text{Cost of Purchase}} \times 365$$

Other Stock Turnover needs to be consistently low as these assets are semi-durable.

Figure 20 Relationship between Sales and Fixed Assets

Ratio Of SALES to FIXED ASSETS

$$\text{Sales to Fixed Assets Ratio} = \frac{\text{SALES}}{\text{FIXED ASSETS}}$$

Most restaurants are extremely good at using their fixed assets. The problems for the Restaurateur usually arise from not owning the costly fixed assets and hemorrhaging high rental or lease costs. This may lead to the use of the fixed assets book value when trying to determine what an asset is worth, regardless of ownership. This is a great example of restaurant efficiency as opposed to profitability. When it comes to the Restaurant Exit plan, the difference needs to be made clear between what is owned and what is not.

Furthermore, boring company law legislation includes a requirement for your restaurant to depreciate its Fixed Assets. Specifically where any asset has a limited useful economic life, the act requires the purchase price or production cost of the asset, less any estimated residual value, to be written off systematically over the assets useful economic life.

Unusually, the Restaurateur can use this ratio to illustrate how much sales can rise if investment in the restaurants fixed assets rises by £1. This may be the proverbial music to potential suitors' ears.

A low ratio, be it positive or negative, that is, the Restaurateur owns the fixed assets or not is likely to indicate the inefficiency of the fixed assets by management. This ratio should be relatively high for your restaurant. The nature of the industry is such that it is considered labour intensive. However, restaurants with high Capital Investments will have a comparatively low ratio. If the dream is to remain alive, your restaurant sales need to be high, all the time.

Sales to Fixed assets ratio shows how the restaurants fixed assets generate sales. There seems to be no better way of showing how the state of the art stove and other fixed assets earn their keep.

According to an old African saying, an elephant never complains that its tusks are too heavy nor should you, the Restaurateur complain if you have a penchant for state of the art fixed assets or pouring money into maintenance and repairs.

Figure 21 Relationship between Sales and Asset Values

RATIO OF SALES TO ASSET VALUE

Sales to Asset Value = $\dfrac{\text{Sales}}{\text{FA + CA}}$ or $\dfrac{\text{Sales}}{\text{NAV}}$

with FA = Fixed Assets
      CA = Current Assets
      NAV = Net Assets Value

$\dfrac{\text{Sales}}{[\text{FA + CA}]}$ $\dfrac{\text{Sales}}{[\text{NAV}]}$

Total Assets Value (Fixed Assets + Current Assets − Current Liabilities)

The Ratio of Sales to Asset value illustrates the ability of the restaurants assets to generate profits for you. This is an assessment of the rate at which asset values such as cookers and ovens are converted into restaurant sales revenue.

'Beware the Ides of Restaurant Financial Analysis'

Using good financial data, calculating Restaurant Financial Ratios is easily done. However, the interpretation of such information lies with the ability and determination of the beholder.

The quality of information that the ratios produce is only as good as the quality of the input material. The later owes more to discipline and determination than it does to knowledge and experience.

In order to draw any relevant conclusions or point in a particular direction, ratios from the Restaurants Financial Analysis need to be compared. They cannot exist as a singularity.

Figure 22 Application of Restaurant Financial Ratios

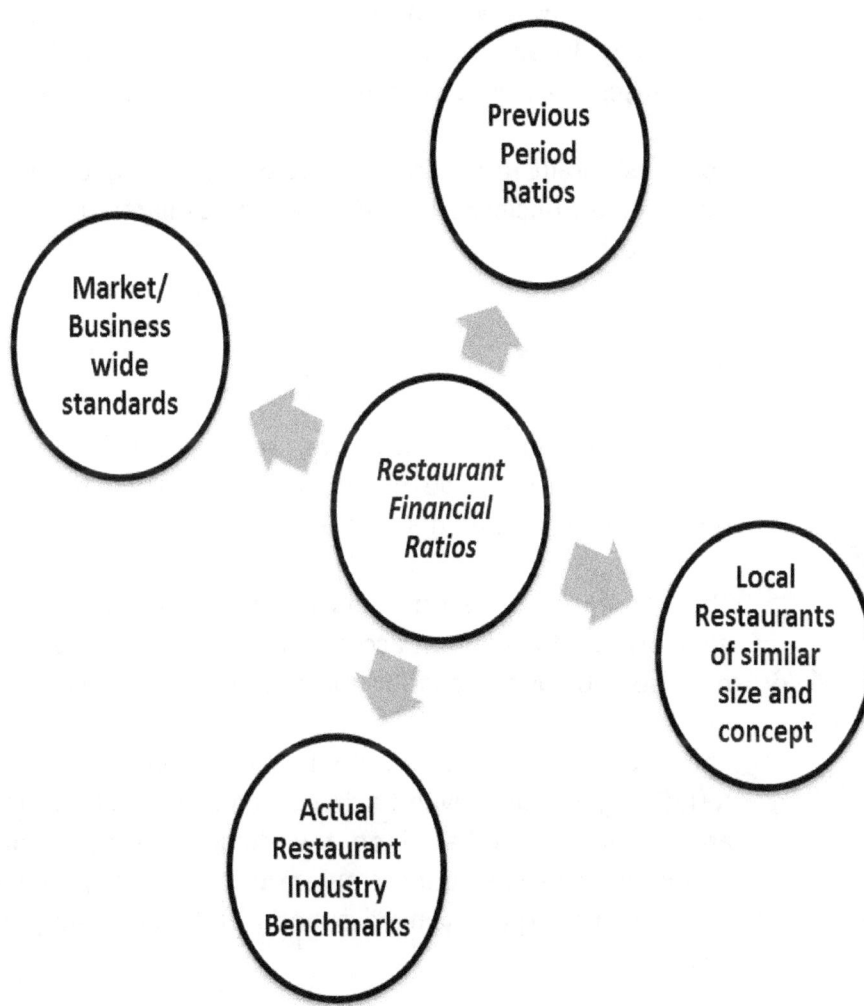

The restaurants accounting ratios are also only a reflection of the changes, or lack thereof, in performance indicators. They do not supply the actual reasons for said results nor do they highlight any causes or account for human errors and human behavior.

Your restaurant ratios are also subject to UK Generally Accepted Accounting principles, UKGAAP, which regulates the preparation of the restaurants final accounts. The principles and policies have inherent options built into them that allow Restaurateurs, or their agents to make choices that may be different to those of their peers.

As a consequence of the above, adjustments for the resulting differences need to be made prior to starting the process of producing the restaurants accounting ratios.

The absence of such adjustments renders the resulting comparison of restaurant accounting ratios not only questionable, but also dubious and possibly misleading at the very least.

The value of all the restaurants financial work would be reduced to nothing and may even further still, have a negative impact on any actions taken based on the dubious ratios. Apart from potentially derailing your restaurant exit plan, any potential suitor may end up experiencing dysphoria and may simply just walk away.

Caveat Emptor. Restaurateurs cannot live on one ratio alone. Subsistence on the interpretation of one ratio or even just two may prove to be ill-judged and fateful.

As an example, the ratio of Sales to Asset value may be great, even impressive. However, a quick calculation of the Current Ratio might produce a very low value, such as 0.198, indicating that your restaurant, as it currently exists, is all but doomed.

It is not the intention to completely destroy the relevance of restaurant accounting ratios. However, as a Restaurateur, one needs to be dutifully reminded that the ratios are normally based on the final accounts of the restaurant. The nature of these is such that the moment they are produced, the instantly become historic.

This immediately affects values, especially costs and in particular Depreciation charge or Bad Debt provision. Subsequently, the profit figure for any comparative restaurant is also affected and no longer reflects a true relative performance.

Unless otherwise stated, as a separate entity, your restaurant business is assumed to continue indefinitely.

As a restaurateur, you should use accounting information and ratios to the extent that they are useful, easy and relevant without the need for 'Einstein-esq' analysis and high costs of detailed activities.

The level of analysis employed by teams of specialists for large corporations is impractical and possibly irrelevant for you as an Independent Restaurateur.

In spite of the above, one-off transactions, special orders and similar irregular activities of a significant amount still have the capacity to skew or distort reports on the true performance of the restaurant.

The exceptional items may need some degree of analysis or adjustment to ensure the accounting ratios are consistently reflective of performance and standardized for effective comparison.

It is not uncommon for notes or explanations to accompany any reports on the restaurant accounting ratios.

Restaurant Investment Appraisal

The majority of independent Restaurateurs are owner-operators who may have gained experience and knowledge while working behind the stoves or busting tables.

The change in economic parameters seems to have reduced the volume of restaurateurs who enter the industry because they just like the idea of owning their own restaurant.

The restaurant industry still has a considerably high failure rate. However, the new breed of 'have-ago-restaurateurs' have a distinct advantage over their predecessors.

Information Technology.

In days past, being a Chef was usually a good enough reason to open Ones' own restaurant. The same goes for the entrepreneurs who 'happen to come into some money'. The only barrier to entry into this industry used to be only as simple as answering the question: 'Surely, how hard could it be?'

In this day and age, most dreamers and incumbents are painfully aware of the misfortune of others and the perils of failing to treat a restaurant venture with sufficient respect as a legitimate Capital project.

Furthermore, as a result of depreciation and evolving business environments, the Restaurateurs also have to apply decision making techniques with regards to upgrades or replacement of plant and machinery. For the restaurant, traditionally this has been the stoves and ovens in addition to dining tables and chairs.

Most operators seek to expand their operations and grow the business. In the majority of cases, it is assumed that the supply of money is not unlimited and therefore opportunities or ideas need to be assessed based on some criteria that have been pre-accepted as a method of evaluating project proposals.

To facilitate your Restaurant Exit Plan, be it to sell the business or whatever route you are comfortable with, it is likely that in order to avoid a usurper, you and a legitimate suitor will employ an evaluation method of some kind.

Perhaps now is a good time to mention that one should always seek professional, insured advice before embarking on any money related adventure. That essentially is what it is, an adventure.

Apparently the Financial Services Authority insist on making it known that the value of any investment, even in a restaurant, could go up and possibly down, unfortunately.

As far as advice for investment appraisal goes, in addition to financial, it may have become mandatory to seek out professional legal advice as well. The Law is constantly changing and sometimes, even if the numbers add up and the heart is in the right place, One could still end up on the wrong side of the law.

The basis of Restaurant Investment Appraisal is sound financial information or data and a few assumptions. Ironically, the former has limitations, which by extension also mean that the resulting methods for restaurant appraisal suffer the same fate.

The later eliminates non-essential influences in order to clearly apply to the practical problems of Restaurant Investment Appraisal.

Figure 23 Restaurant Appraisal Assumptions

The Restaurant Appraisal Assumptions

 Future Costs and Income accurately estimated, prefarably based on accounting records

 The Cost of Capital for the Restaurateur is the cost or mar rate for borrowing money to fi Investment

 When a project is selected, there will be no obsticles to slow down the completion of the project. For example, Staff shortages or lack of material resouces

 The impact of inflation and TAX assumed to be neutral

Figure 24 Restaurant Investment Appraisal Techniques

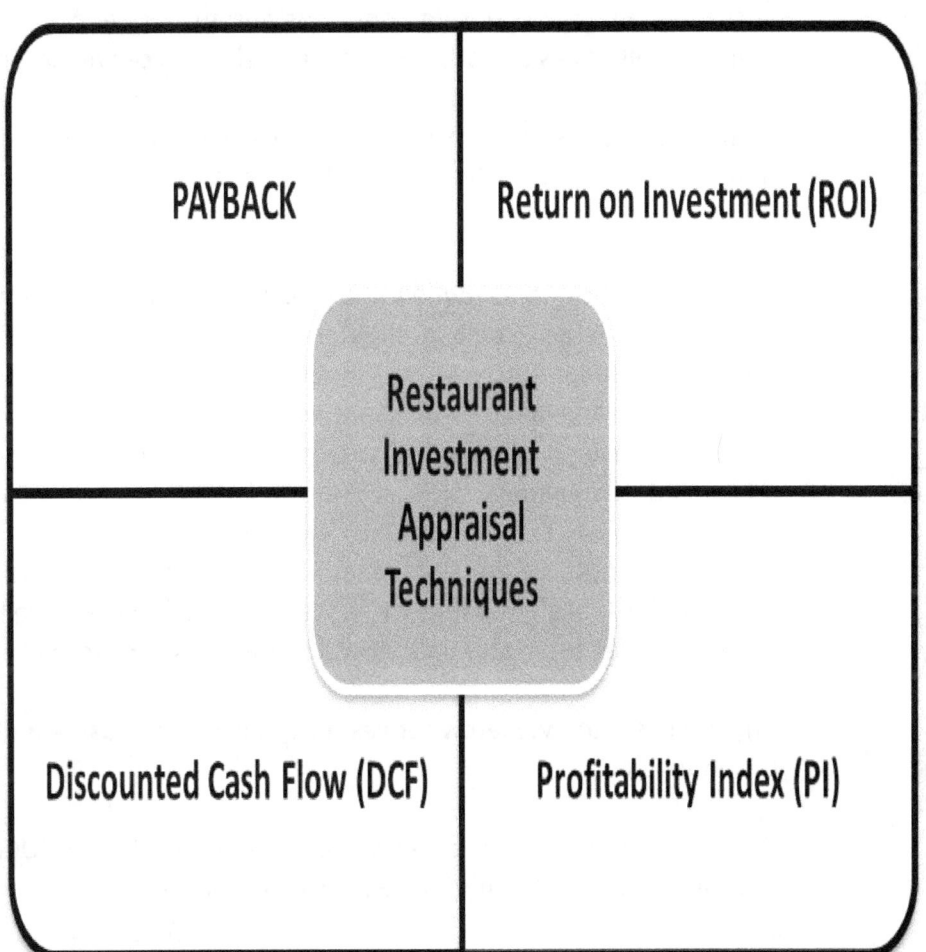

Only one technique or method is sufficient enough to help in the decision making process. However, at times money may be in short supply or projects may be mutually exclusive. The later arises when by choosing one restaurant project; the act automatically rules out or precludes the selection of any others.

From the results, the restaurants investment projects may be ranked in order of profitability and a selection made of the best choice.

The best method to use when it comes to restaurant investments depends to a large extent on the Restaurateurs desired End Game for the Exit Plan.
Initially, knowing where you want to end up is a good starting point because it makes it incredibly easy to choose the appropriate technique.

However, it pays to understand at the initial introductory phase what options are available or what each technique entails as nothing is ever set in stone as far as the future is concerned.

Anyone likely to evaluate your restaurant is likely to use a method of some sort.

If the intention is to use either the Discounted Cash Flow (DCF) or Profitability Index (PI), please seek professional advice.

Restaurant Payback Technique

For the Restaurateur or Investor with time and capital recovery or capital return as major factors, this may be the best technique.

Payback focuses on the time period over which the Initial Investment outlay on the restaurant project or its assets can be recovered from the cash generated by the restaurant or project.

Good accounting records will highlight the cost and corresponding Net cash inflow over the future time periods. If the choice is between different investment projects, then normally the one with the shortest payback period is selected.

This simple technique allows for the easy calculation of payback periods. Commercial Banks seem to be reluctant to lend to Restaurateurs, the resulting scarcity of cash makes it not only sensible but also appealing to evaluate the restaurants projects based on payback periods.

Apparently most restaurants fail within the first 3 years or so. Therefore, using the Payback Technique is rather an adept way of evaluating whether the initial investment will be recovered within the estimated payback period before the statistical mark at which most restaurants go 'belly up'.

The longer into the uncertain future the plan is projected to go, the greater the uncertainty and risk to you the Restaurateur, or a qualified buyer/investor.

The Payback technique places special emphasis on the early time periods of the project providing a clearer assessment.

However, as a result of one of the key assumptions of the techniques of Restaurant Investment Appraisal, Payback does not take into account the Time Value of Money (TVM).

TVM is described in greater detail in *Restaurant Financial Management: Introduction to Accounting and Finance for Independent Restaurants.*

In a nutshell, TVM assumes that the Restaurateurs £1 received in a future time period is worth more than £1 received now. This Payback technique ignores TVM aspects and assets that all £1's are equal, at all times.

Furthermore, the Payback technique cares not for any cash flows after the payback period nor does it consider the overall profitability of the project.

Return on Restaurant Investment Technique

This technique is more about profitability than it is about time. It measures the return on Restaurant investment in much the same way as the Return on Capital Employed.

The latter is as described earlier, a financial profitability ratio where the restaurant net profit is expressed as a percentage of the Capital employed.

Rest assured, anyone looking at acquiring your restaurant business will prioritise looking after themselves and their money. They may even require you to relinquish your own priorities' to some extent.

Normally, this technique uses the average investment in the restaurant, rather than the total initial investment as well as the average annual profit to calculate the Return on Investment (ROI).

Figure 25 Return on Investment

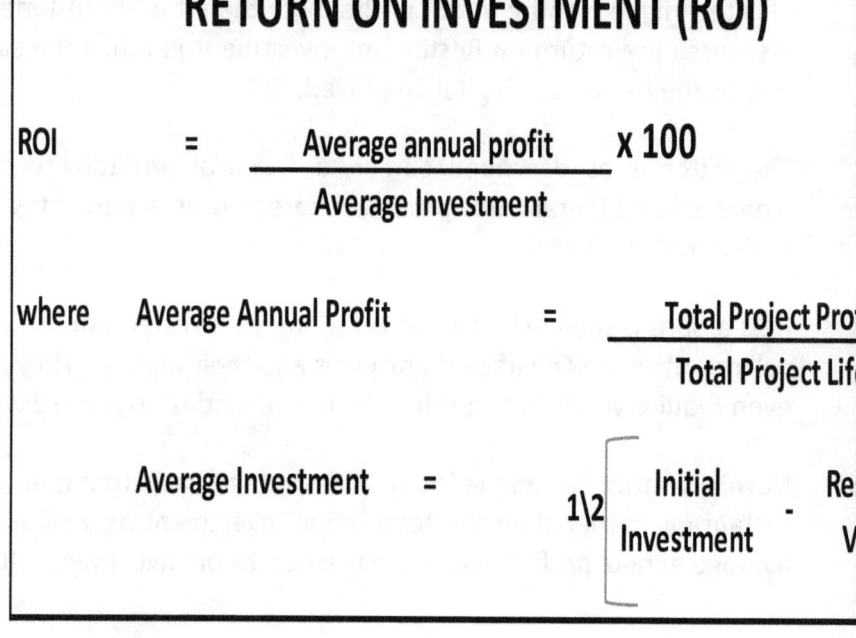

Residual Value or Scrap Value is the estimated market value of the restaurant project or asset at the end of its desirable working life.

If, unfortunately the project or asset has no Residual or Scrap Value, the Average Investment will automatically be half the initial investment.

The projects are usually ranked on the greatness of their ROI and a clear selection made.

As quite clearly demonstrated, this is a fairly simple technique to understand and fairly easy to calculate too. The emphasis is on measuring profitability and very meaningful when it comes to assessing the value of a Restaurant Investment project.

In spite of the clear benefits of the ROI technique, it falls short and does not take into consideration cash inflows, outflows or their important timings. This is very important as restaurants do not usually survive an episode of acute cash shortage, however brief.

In conclusion, like its predecessor, ROI also chooses not to consider the Time Value of Money (TVM).

Parting Note

Bear in mind when seeking advice on your Restaurant Exit Plan that it is assumed that your restaurant business will continue indefinitely, all things being equal.

You also have to be prudent and not overstate the restaurants worth or value. Within your Exit Plan, please do not overstate the restaurants profit by not allowing for all expenses incurred during that accounting period. The same goes for understating losses.

Please be disciplined and vigilant to ensure that all the restaurants expenses incurred during as accounting period must be charged accurately during the corresponding accounting period.

All this appears obvious but knowledgeable suitors will sift through your restaurant accounts with a pair of chopsticks or fish tweezers until they know everything there is to know or find out about the restaurant. More importantly, they will also know about you, come up with a plan and then maybe take a seat at the negotiating table, armed and ready.

Caveat Emptor as they say, perhaps Caveat Venditor.

'Bon Chance'.

www.ingramcontent.com/pod-product-compliance
Lightning Source LLC
Chambersburg PA
CBHW070427180526
45158CB00017B/905